The new boy

Written by Narinder Dhami

Illustrated by Jamie Smith

Heinemann

Warwick St. Mary's
R.C. Primary School

Sally and Robin were twins.
One day they were looking for
their old cat, Moggy, when they saw
a big van. Then they saw a boy by
the van. He looked sad.

'Look, Robin,' said Sally, 'someone has come to live in that house.'

'Let's go and see,' said Robin.

They got off their bikes and went over to the van.

Robin and Sally went up to the boy.
'I'm Sally and this is Robin. Do you want to play with us?'
'No,' said the boy, 'I don't want to play with you.'

'We only want to be friends,' said Sally.
'I don't want to be friends with you,'
said the boy. 'I want my old friends.
I want to go back to our old house.'

Just then Moggy jumped down from a wall and went into the boy's garden.
'That's our cat, Moggy,' said Sally.
'I don't like cats,' said the boy. 'Get him out of here.'

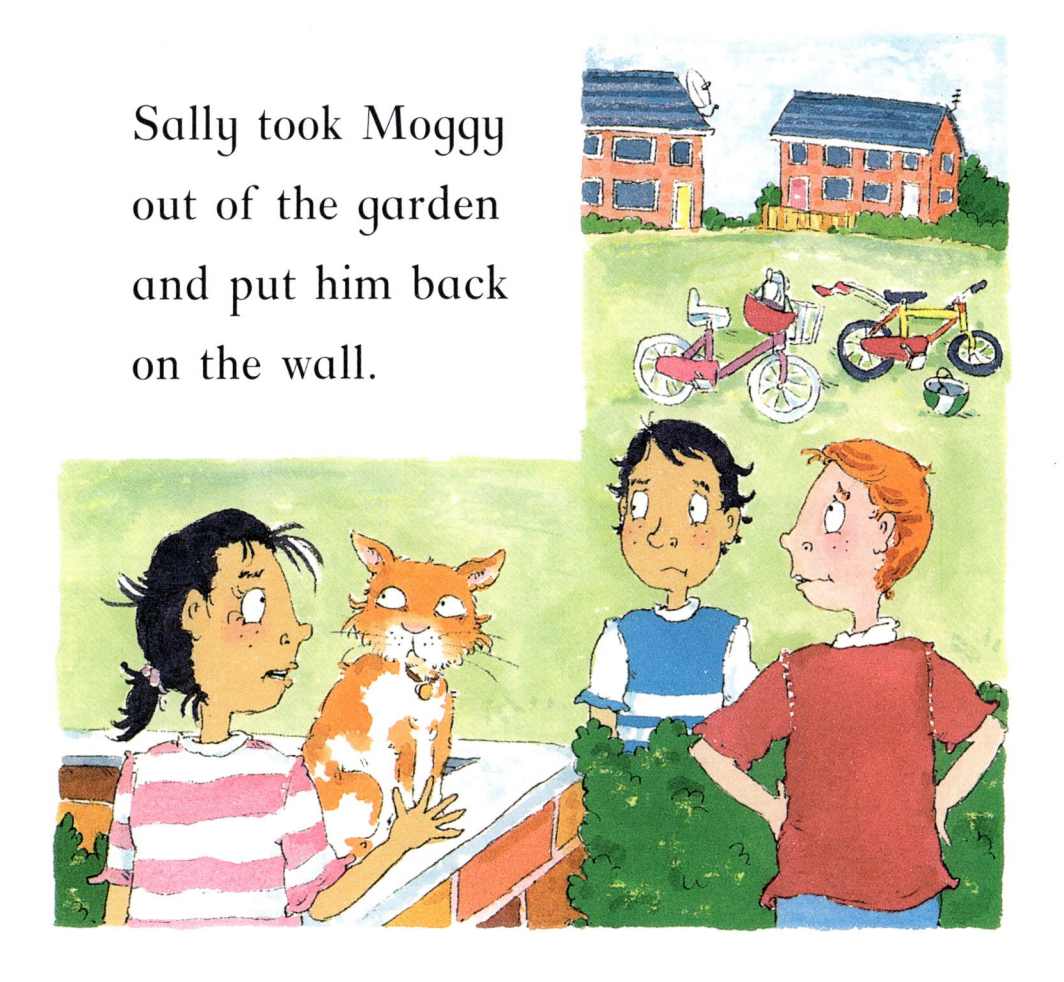

Sally took Moggy
out of the garden
and put him back
on the wall.

'Come on, Robin. Let's go and play
on our bikes again,' she said.
'Your bikes are no good,' said the boy.
'My bike is much bigger and faster
than yours.'

That made Sally cross.

'So you think you can go faster than us, do you?' she said.

'Yes, I'll show you,' said the boy, and he went off to get his bike.

'I don't like him much,' said Robin.
'I don't like him at all!' said Sally.
'I'll show him that my bike can go faster than his!'

The boy came back with his bike.
It was bigger than Sally's bike
and it looked as if it could go much
faster too.

Sally and the boy got on their bikes and Robin called out,

'One – two – three – GO!'

'Come on, Sally!' Robin called.

Sally tried to catch up with the boy but he was going much too fast for her.

Just then Moggy jumped down from the wall. He sat down on the path and went to sleep.

Moggy didn't see the boy coming on his bike.

'Oh no!' said Robin. 'He's going to run into Moggy.'

Then the boy looked up and saw Moggy on the path. He pulled on his brakes and Moggy ran away.

But then the boy fell off his bike and cut his knee.

Sally and Robin ran over to him.

'You would have been first if you hadn't stopped,' said Robin.

'Yes,' said the boy, 'but I didn't want to hurt your cat.'

Then the boy said, 'I'm sorry I was cross before. Can we be friends now?'
'Yes,' said Sally and Robin, and they all went off to play on their bikes.